# The Unofficial

# Harry Potter Cookbook

## 250 Amazing Recipes for Wizards and Muggles

*Muriel Vandorn*

# Table of Contents

# Recipe 1 -   Special Pudding

This pudding is best to serve on Halloween parties, and special Potter inspired theme parties. It is cooked well on simmering water. Unlike ordinary pudding, it is rich in dried fruits, apple, almonds, and crumbs which gives it a crunchy texture.

**Serving Size:** 12

**Prep Time:** 10 minutes

**Total Prep Time:** 7 hours

**Ingredients:**

• 1-ounce candied peel (mixed varieties, finely chopped)

- 1-pound mixed dried fruit
- 1 Tbsp. orange zest
- 1 small apple (cooking apple, peeled, cored and chopped finely)
- 2 Tbsp. orange juice
- ½ Tbsp. lemon zest
- 4 Tbsp. brandy
- 1 Tbsp. lemon juice
- 1 tsp. mixed spice (level, ground)
- 2 ounces flour (self-raising, sifted)
- 4 ounces suet vegetarian, shredded
- 1 ½ tsp. cinnamon (ground)
- 4 ounces breadcrumbs (white, fresh)
- 4 ounces brown sugar (dark, soft)
- 2 large eggs (fresh)
- 1-ounce almonds (whole, shelled, roughly chopped)

**Directions:**

1. Grease a 2.5-pint pudding basin with butter.

2. Mix candied peel with apple, dried fruits, lemon juice and orange juice in a mixing bowl.

3. Stir in brandy and cover the bowl. Marinate overnight.

4. Mix flour with cinnamon and mixed spice in a bowl.

5. Stir in sugar, lemon, orange zest, nuts, suet, and breadcrumbs. Mix well.

6. Add marinated dried fruits and mix well.

7. Beat eggs in a bowl and stir in all the dry ingredients.

8. Transfer the mixture to the pudding basin and cook over simmering water for 7 hours.

9. Stir well after every 15 minutes.

10. Allow it to cool then serve.

# Recipe 2 - Steak and Kidney Pieces

Throughout his adventures through the series, there are numerous occasions where Harry enjoys these pies. Apparently, they are so delicious, Harry relishes about them frequently.

**Serving Sizes:** 6 servings

**Cooking Time:** 2 hours and 15 minutes

**Ingredients:**

- 1 pound of ground beef
- 1, 10 ounces steak, sliced in cubes

- 1 ounce of all-purpose flour
- 4 ½ ounces of forest mushrooms, trimmed and thinly sliced
- 1 lemon, juice only
- 2 tablespoons of vegetable oil
- 1 ounce of butter
- 1 onion, chopped
- 2 tablespoons of Worcestershire sauce
- 2 tablespoons of tomato paste
- ½ cup of dark beef
- 1 cup of low sodium beef broth
- 1 teaspoon of thyme leaves, chopped
- 1 bay leaf
- 6 ounces of puff pastry
- 7 ounces of short crust pastry
- 1 egg yolk

**Directions:**

1. In a Ziploc bag, add in the steak cubes and ground beef. Add in the all-purpose flour. Seal the bag and toss well to mix.

2. In a saucepan set over medium heat, add in the vegetable oil and butter. Once the butter melts, add

in the onion. Cook for 5 minutes or until soft. Transfer into a bowl.

3. Add the ground beef and steak into the saucepan. Cook for 8 to 10 minutes or until browned. Add the onion back into the saucepan. Add in the Worcestershire sauce, tomato paste, dark beef, low sodium beef broth, sliced mushrooms, chopped thyme leaves and bay leaf. Stir well to mix.

4. Allow to come to a boil. Lower the heat to low and cook for 1 hour. Remove the bay leaf.

5. Preheat the oven to 350 degrees.

6. Roll out the puff pastry and short crust pastry. Line 6 pie plates with the short crust pastry. Trim the edges. Pour the filling into the crust. Cover each of the pies with the puff pastry. Slice slits into the surface of the puff pastry for venting. Brush with the egg yolk.

7. Place into the oven to bake for 45 minutes or until golden.

8. Remove and cool for 15 minutes before serving.

# Recipe 3 - Breaded Pork Chops

This was a huge hit at the Yule Ball and now you can have it as a huge hit your home. Serve with a salad for the tastiest results.

**Serving Sizes:** 4 servings

**Cooking Time:** 15 minutes

**Ingredients:**

- 4, 6-ounce pork chops
- Dash of salt and black pepper
- 1 cup of all-purpose flour
- 2 eggs, beaten
- 2 cups of seasoned breadcrumbs

- Vegetable oil, as needed

**Directions:**

1. Pat dry the pork chops with a few paper towels. Season with a dash of salt and black pepper.

2. In a bowl, add in the seasoned pork chops. In a separate bowl, add in the all-purpose flour. In a third separate bowl, add in the beaten eggs.

3. Dredge the pork chops in the flour mix until coated on all sides. Dip into the beaten eggs and roll in the breadcrumbs until coated.

4. Place a skillet over medium to high heat. Add in 1 to 3 inches of vegetable oil. Heat the vegetable oil until it reaches 350 degrees. Once hot, add in the coated pork chops. Cook for 5 minutes on each side or until browned and cooked through.

5. Transfer onto a plate lined with paper towels to drain.

6. Serve immediately.

# Recipe 4 - Golden Snitch Cake

For great events and special birthday parties, this cake is the best surprise you can easily arrange at home. Inspired from original Golden snitch this cake is loaded with yellow icing. Add paper wings to the sides, and it will look as real as the Harry Potter series. To add more details, make swirling patterns on the outer layer of icing using a piping tip.

**Serving Size:** 10

**Prep Time:** 20 minutes

**Total Prep Time:** 32 minutes

**Ingredients:**

**For Cake:**

- 2/3 cup coconut flour

- ½ cup cocoa powder
- ½ tsp. baking soda
- ½ tsp. salt
- ½ cup plain Greek yogurt
- 3/4 cup honey
- 6 eggs
- ½ cup water
- 1 Tbsp. vanilla extract

**For the butterscotch frosting:**

- 3 egg whites
- ½ cup 2 Tbsp. coconut sugar
- 1 cup butter,
- 1 tsp. vanilla extract
- 2 Tbsp. butterscotch schnapps
- pinch of salt
- 4 drops yellow food coloring
- gold pearl dust

**For the wings:**

- template for tracing
- 1 large piece of scrapbook paper (silver or gold)
- 2 lollipop sticks
- hot glue

**Directions:**

**For chocolate cake:**

1. Set the oven to 350 degrees F.

2. Grease two ovenproof glass bowls with oil.

3. Mix coconut flour with baking soda, salt and cocoa powder in a bowl.

4. Beat yogurt with honey in a mixer until smooth. Gradually add eggs while beating.

5. Stir in vanilla and water and mix well until smooth.

6. Slowly stir in flour mixture and mix until combined.

7. Divide the batter into two bowls and bake for 32 minutes.

8. Let the cakes to cool and remove from the glass bowls.

9. Wrap them in foil sheets and refrigerate for 2 hours.

**For the butterscotch frosting:**

10. Meanwhile, boil 2 inches of water in a saucepan.

11. Whisk egg whites with sugar in a glass bowl and place it on the simmering water.

12. Mix well until sugar is dissolved.

13. Beat the mixture until foamy.

14. Add butter then blend on low speed until mixed.

15. Stir in yellow food color and mix well to get a golden color.

**For the wings:**

16. Make four wings using scrapbook paper by cutting into the wing shapes.

17. Stick two wings together while putting a lollipop stick at the center to insert.

**To assemble:**

18. Unwrap the cakes and place one cake on the cake board with its round side down.

19. Top this cake with a dollop of frosting and place the other cake with its flat side down.

20. Coat the entire cake with one layer of frosting evenly.

21. Refrigerate the cake for 20 minutes.

22. Again, the coat the cake with the frosting and refrigerate for 20 minutes.

23. Insert wings on the sides.

24. Serve.

# Recipe 5 - Homemade Pumpkin Pasties

Even if you can't visit Hogwarts as a muggle, you can enjoy these pumpkin pasties fresh off the Hogwarts Express trolley in the comfort of your own home.

**Serving Sizes:** 8 servings

**Cooking Time:** 55 minutes

**Ingredients:**

- 7.5 ounces of pureed pumpkin
- 1 Tablespoon of butter
- 1 teaspoon of powdered cinnamon
- ½ teaspoon of pumpkin pie seasoning

- ¼ teaspoon of powdered allspice
- 2 tablespoons of white sugar
- 1 pack of pie dough
- All-purpose flour, for dusting
- 1 egg, beaten and for egg wash

**Directions:**

1. Preheat the oven to 400 degrees. Place a sheet of parchment paper onto two baking sheets.

2. In a bowl, add in the pureed pumpkin, butter, white sugar, powdered cinnamon, pumpkin pie seasoning and powdered allspice. Stir well to mix.

3. Dust a flat surface lightly with flour. Roll the pie dough until 1/8 inch in thickness. Slice into 4-inch circles.

4. Add a tablespoon of the pumpkin mix into the center of each circle. Fold over to cover and crimp the edges to seal. Repeat and transfer onto the baking sheets.

5. Brush the top of the pasties with the egg wash.

6. Place into the oven to bake for 15 to 20 minutes or until golden.

7. Transfer onto a wire rack to cool for 5 minutes before serving.

# Recipe 6 - Cheese and Pretzel Broomsticks

We can't even imagine a wizard without a broomstick. That is why this simple recipe brings cheese broomsticks to your special menu. Making use of sheer creativity, you can turn your cheese slices and stored pretzels into something so fascinating and delicious. Serve them either a snack or an appetizer.

**Serving Size:** 12

**Prep Time:** 10 minutes

**Total Prep Time:** 0 minutes

**Ingredients:**

- 12 stick pretzels
- 6 cheese slices

- 3 shallots, green parts only

**Directions:**

1. Cut the cheese slices in half and make fringes at one end of each slice.

2. Wrap the fringed slices one end of the pretzel with fringes on the other end.

3. Slice thin strips out of the green part of the shallot.

4. Secure the cheese wraps using these thin strips.

5. Serve.

# Recipe 7 - Homemade Sugar Biscuits

This is another one of Hagrid's famous treats that he serves to Harry and his friends after Harry survived his fight with Voldemort after the Triwizard tournament.

**Serving Sizes:** 64 servings

**Cooking Time:** 2 hours and 20 minutes

**Ingredients:**

- 3 cups of all-purpose flour
- ½ teaspoon of baking soda
- ¼ teaspoon of salt
- 16 tablespoons of butter
- 1 ½ cups of white sugar
- 2 eggs

- 1 ½ teaspoon of pure vanilla
- Turbinado sugar, for sprinkling

**Directions:**

1. In a bowl, add the baking soda, all-purpose flour and dash of salt. Stir well to mix.

2. In a separate bowl, add in the butter and white sugar. Beat with an electric mixer until fluffy in consistency. Add in the eggs and pure vanilla. Beat well until creamy in consistency.

3. Add in the flour mix and continue to beat until a dough forms.

4. Divide the dough in half and shape each piece into a disc. Cover in sheet of plastic wrap and set into the fridge to chill for 2 hours.

5. Preheat the oven to 350 degrees. Place a sheet of parchment paper onto two baking sheets.

6. Roll the dough pieces until ¼ inch in thickness. Slice out cookies that are 3 inches in size and place onto the baking sheets.

7. Sprinkle the turbinado sugar over the cookies.

8. Place into the oven to bake for 10 to 12 minutes or until gold. Remove and set aside to cool completely before serving.

# Recipe 8 -   Neville's favourite dessert

## Ingredients:

- 150g of flour
- 1 teaspoon of yeast
- Salt to taste
- 5 tablespoons of butter
- 65g of sugar
- 90mL of milk
- Lemon peel
- 100g of raisins

**Directions:**

Combine the sifted flour, yeast, salt, butter and sugar using an electric mixer. Then add the milk, lemon and raisins (soaked in rum for a few minutes). Move everything in a container with a lid that can be boiled, in my case an empty jar of jam. Place jar inside a pot full of boiling water. Cook for 90 minutes. Serve lukewarm

**Ingredients for vanilla cream:**

- 125mL of cream
- 125mL of milk
- 2 yolks
- vanilla to taste
- 1 tablespoon of starch
- 30g of sugar

Combine all the ingredients in a pot and mix until a homogeneous mixture is obtained. Turn on the heat and cook the cream on low heat, without bringing it to boil. When is start thickening, turn the heat off. Pour the cream over the pudding.

# Recipe 9 - Double Chocolate Cauldron Cakes

Cauldron cake is particularly popular in the Harry Potter menu for their adorable outlook and amazing flavor. Mothers all around the world are going extra miles to get its perfect recipe to surprise their little harry fans on special celebrations. They contain the goodness of chocolate and the cakes and serve as a nourishing dessert for every table.

**Serving Size:** 6

**Prep Time:** 10 minutes

**Total Prep Time:** 20 minutes

**Ingredients:**

## For the Cakes

- 2 cups all-purpose flour
- 3/4 cup cocoa powder
- 1 ½ tsp. baking powder
- ½ tsp. baking soda
- 1 tsp. salt
- ½ cup canola oil
- 2 cups sugar
- 1 egg
- 1 tsp. vanilla
- 1 cup milk
- 1 cup semi-sweet chocolate chips

## For the Filling

- ½ cup butter
- ½ cup sugar
- ½ cup milk
- 4 ½ tsp. all-purpose flour
- 4 ½ tsp. powdered chocolate milk mix
- ½ tsp. vanilla

## For the Frosting

- 1 cup butter
- 4 cups confectioners' sugar
- 1 ¼ cups cocoa powder
- ½ tsp. vanilla
- ¼ to ½ cup milk

## Directions:

## Cake:

1. Set your oven to 350 degrees F. Layer a muffin tray with paper liners.

2. Mix flour with baking powder, cocoa, salt and baking powder in a bowl.

3. Beat oil with sugar in a mixing bowl. Whisk in egg and vanilla.

4. Gradually add flour mixture and milk alternatively while blending.

5. Fold in chocolate chips and add 2 Tbsp. of the batter into each muffin cup.

6. Bake for about 20 minutes.

## To make the filling:

7. Mix milk with chocolate drink mix and flour in a saucepan over medium-high heat.

8. Stir cook until it thickens then turn off the heat. Allow it to cool.

9. Blend sugar and butter in an electric mixer until fluffy.

10. Stir in vanilla and milk mixture.

To make the frosting:

11. Blend butter with sugar in a mixer and stir in cocoa and vanilla.

12. Gradually add milk while beating until fluffy.

**Assembling:**

13. Dip the base of each muffin cake into melted chocolate.

14. Carve a groove at the center of each muffin base.

15. Divide the filling into each groove and top each with frosting.

16. Make cauldron handles by piping melted chocolate over parchment paper into U shape.

17. Allow them to cool and dry.

18. Fix these handles in the cauldrons and serve.

# Recipe 10 - Butterbeer Cake

If you have to celebrate a Harry Potter fans birthday, then this is the perfect cake for you to prepare. It is so delicious, I guarantee you will want to make it for everybody's birthday.

**Serving Sizes:** 12 servings

**Cooking Time:** 1 hour and 30 minutes

**Ingredients for the cake:**

- 2 cups of cake flour
- 1 ½ teaspoon of baking powder
- ½ teaspoon of baking soda
- Dash of salt

- ½ cup of butter, soft

- ¾ cup of light brown sugar

- 3 eggs

- 1 cup of buttermilk

- 2 teaspoons of pure vanilla

- 2 teaspoons of butter flavoring

- 1 Tablespoon of caramel syrup

**Ingredients for the frosting:**

- ¼ cup + ½ cup of butter, soft

- 3 tablespoons of all-purpose flour

- ¾ cup of whole milk

- 1 ½ teaspoon of pure vanilla

- ½ cup of powdered sugar

- ¼ cup of light brown sugar

**Ingredients for the ganache:**

- 1, 11-ounce bag of butterscotch chips

- 1 cup of heavy whipping cream

- ½ teaspoon of salt

**Directions:**

1. Preheat the oven to 350 degrees. Line a cake pan with a sheet of parchment paper. Grease with cooking spray and dust lightly with flour.

2. Prepare the cake. In the bowl of a stand mixer, add in the cake flour, dash of salt, baking powder and soda. Stir well to mix. Add in the light brown sugar. Stir well to mix. Add in the soft butter. Beat on the lowest setting until crumbly in consistency.

3. In a separate bowl, add in the eggs, buttermilk, pure vanilla, butter flavoring and caramel syrup. Stir well to mix. Pour into the flour mix. Continue to mix until smooth in consistency.

4. Pour into the cake pan. Place into the oven to bake for 25 to 30 minutes or until baked through. Remove and set aside to cool on a wire rack completely.

5. Prepare the frosting. In a saucepan set over medium to high heat, add in ¼ cup of butter. Once the butter becomes browned, add in the all-purpose flour. Whisk until smooth in consistency. Allow to come to a boil. Add in the pure vanilla. Whisk well to mix. Set aside to cool.

6. In a separate bowl, add in the remaining ½ cup of butter, powdered sugar and light brown sugar. Beat with an electric mixer until creamy in consistency. Add the saucepan mix into this mix. Continue to beat until evenly mixed.

7. Prepare the ganache. In a bowl, add in the butterscotch chips, heavy whipping cream and dash of salt. Microwave on the highest setting for 30

seconds to 1 minute or until melted. Whisk until smooth in consistency.

8. Spread the frosting onto the cake, spreading evenly on the sides and top.

9. Pour the ganache over the top of the cake.

10. Slice and serve.

# Recipe 11 - Chocolate Frogs

These are simple chocolate frogs which you can prepare in just a few minutes. With simple steps and basic ingredients, you can enjoy peanut butter filled chocolate toads at home. Chill well before serving to enjoy the best of its flavor.

**Serving Size:** 8

**Prep Time:** 10 minutes

**Total Prep Time:** 02 minutes

**Ingredients:**

- 1-pound milk chocolate

## Peanut Butter Filling:

- ½ cup natural peanut butter
- ¼ cup + 2 Tbsp. confectioners' sugar
- 1/8 tsp. salt
- Special equipment: frog shaped mold

## Directions:

1. Melt chocolate in a bowl by heating in the microwave for 30 seconds.

2. Pour this melt into the frog molds. Allow it to cool.

3. Combine all the filling ingredients in a glass bowl.

4. Stuff the chocolate molds with the filling and press it gently into the molds.

5. Refrigerate for 30 minutes.

6. Serve.

# Recipe 12 - Butterbeer Cupcakes

These delicious cupcakes are some of the best kind of cupcakes that you will ever make. Made with a brown sugar and vanilla flavor, this is a great treat to make whenever you are craving something sweet.

**Serving Sizes:** 18 servings

**Cooking Time:** 50 minutes

**Ingredients for the cupcakes:**

- 1 box of yellow cake mix
- 3 eggs
- ½ cup of vegetable oil
- 1 cup of vanilla crème soda

- ¼ cup of light brown sugar
- 1, 3.4-ounce pack of butterscotch pudding mix

**Ingredients for the frosting:**

- ½ cup of butter, soft
- 2 tablespoons of butterscotch sauce, extra for drizzling
- ¼ cup of light brown sugar
- ½ teaspoon of butter extract
- 1 teaspoon of pure vanilla
- 3 ½ to 4 cups of powdered sugar
- ¼ cup of heavy whipping cream

**Directions:**

1. Preheat the oven to 350 degrees. Place paper muffin liners into a muffin pan.

2. Prepare the cupcakes. In a bowl, add in the yellow cake mix, eggs, vegetable oil, vanilla crème soda, light brown sugar and butterscotch pudding mix. Stir well until smooth in consistency.

3. Pour into the muffin pan, filling each cup ¾ of the way full.

4. Place into the oven to bake for 15 to 20 minutes or until baked through. Remove and set aside to cool.

5. Prepare the frosting. In the bowl of a stand mixer, add in the soft butter, butterscotch sauce, light brown sugar, butter extract, pure vanilla, powdered sugar and heavy whipping cream. Beat on the highest setting until fluffy in consistency.

6. Pipe the frosting onto the cupcakes.

7. Drizzle the extra butterscotch sauce over the top.

# Recipe 13 - Slughorn's Secret

## Ingredients:

- 500 gr - Type 1 White Flour
- Warm water
- Extra virgin olive oil
- 1 Sachet - Yeast
- 15 - Elderberry flowers
- salt

## Directions:

1. The first thing to know about Elderflower Schiacciata is that you need a bit of sensitivity:

similarly to bread, you have to "feel" the dough to learn to understand when it is ready.

2. First of all, clean the elderberry flowers: do not wash them with water, because they would lose all the pollen and the flavor: just eliminate the hardest stems. Then place the flour on the shelf, add salt, yeast, a little water and oil and start kneading. When the mixture starts to have a little consistency, add the elderberry flowers and keep kneading.

3. You will have to knead vigorously for a good moment, until you get a firm, elastic and non-sticky dough. If it does not stay together, add a drop of water, if it is too liquid, add a little flour.

4. At this point, put the dough in a large bowl, cover it with a cloth and let it rest in a warm place for at least an hour. When it becomes swollen and soft, you can start cooking it.

5. Smear a baking sheet with olive oil and spread the dough over it (it must maintain a thickness of about 1 to 2 centimeters). Prick it with a fork, smear it with oil, sprinkle with coarse salt and bake for 30/40 minutes in a preheated oven at 180 ° (ventilated).

6. Check the consistency with a fork: it's ideal when the flatbread is neither too dry nor too soft. When it is ready, take it out of the oven and let it cool down a little. Your secret recipe is ready!

# Recipe 14 - Classic Roast Beef

If there is a dish that is often served up in the Great Hall, it is this delicious dish. Serve with mashed potatoes or pumpkin bread for the real Harry Potter experience.

**Serving Sizes:** 8 servings

**Cooking Time:** 1 hour and 30 minutes

**Ingredients:**

- 1, 4 to 5-pound rib roast
- 3 tablespoons of salt
- 1 Tablespoon of black pepper

**Directions:**

1. Heat the oven to 375 degrees. Grease a roasting rack with cooking spray. Place into a roasting pan.

2. Rinse the roast beef and pat dry with a few paper towels. Season with a dash of salt and black pepper.

3. Place the roast beef into the roasting pan.

4. Place into the oven to bake for 1 hour and 20 minutes. Remove and cover with a sheet of aluminum foil. Set aside to rest for 15 to 20 minutes.

5. Carve and serve.

# Recipe 15 - Fried Tomatoes

After dealing with dementors on the train, Harry and his friends recover from their encounter the next morning with this delicious breakfast dish. One bite of these tomatoes and you will also become hooked.

**Serving Sizes:** 4 servings

**Cooking Time:** 10 minutes

**Ingredients:**

- 3 tablespoons of vegetable oil

- 2 tomatoes, ripe and sliced thinly

- All-purpose flour, for dredging

- Dash of salt and black pepper

- Toast, for serving

**Directions:**

1. In a skillet set over medium to high heat, add in the vegetable oil.

2. Dredge the tomato slices in the all-purpose flour until coated on both sides. Place into the hot oil. Fry for 3 to 5 minutes on each side or until golden.

3. Transfer onto a plate lined with paper towels to drain.

4. Season with a dash of salt and black pepper.

5. Serve immediately with toast.

# Recipe 16 - Bangers and Mash

This is a classic British dish that teens and children alike enjoy. In the United States it is referred to as sausages and mash and will become one of your favorite dishes.

**Serving Sizes:** 6 servings

**Cooking Time:** 1 hour and 10 minutes

**Ingredients for the bangers:**

- ½ pound of ground veal
- ½ pound of lean ground pork
- 1 cup of breadcrumbs

- 1 teaspoon of grated lemon zest

- 1 teaspoon of salt

- ¼ teaspoon of powdered nutmeg

- 1 teaspoon of powdered sage

- 1/8 teaspoon of dried marjoram

- 1/8 teaspoon of powdered thyme

- ¼ teaspoon of black pepper

- 2 egg yolks

- 2 tablespoons of butter, soft

**Ingredients for the mash:**

- 6 potatoes, peeled and cut into quarters

- 2 teaspoons of salt

- 4 tablespoons of butter, soft

- 1 cup of whole milk

- Dash of black pepper

**Ingredients for the gravy:**

- 3 tablespoons of vegetable oil

- 1 onion, chopped

- 3 tablespoons of all-purpose flour

- 2 cups of low sodium chicken broth

- Dash of salt

**Directions:**

1. Prepare the bangers. In a bowl, add in all of the ingredients for the bangers except for 2 tablespoons of butter. Stir well to mix. Shape into patties.

2. In a skillet set over medium to high heat, add in the butter. Add in the banger patties. Cook for 5 minutes on each side or until browned. Transfer onto a plate lined with paper towels to drain. Set aside.

3. Prepare the mash. In a pot set over medium to high heat, fill with water. Allow to come to a boil. Add in the potatoes. Lower the heat to low. Boil for 25 minutes or until the potatoes are soft. Drain and add into a bowl.

4. In the bowl, add in the dash of salt, butter, whole milk and dash of black pepper. Mash well until smooth in consistency.

5. Prepare the gravy. In a saucepan set over medium heat, add in the onions. Cook for 5 minutes or until soft. Continue to cook for 25 minutes or until the onions are caramelized. Add in the all-purpose flour. Whisk to mix. Add in the chicken broth and cover. Cook for 5 minutes or until thick in consistency.

6. Place the banger patties onto a serving plate. Add a mound of mash and pour the gravy over the top.

7. Serve.

# Recipe 17 - Hogwarts Pie

## Ingredients:

- Eggs 1
- 125 g sugar
- 125 g Butter
- 1 Vanillin sachet
- 280 g flour (type 00)
- 8 g Powder for baking
- 1 pinch of salt

*Stuffing:*

- to taste Apricot jam
- to taste strawberry jam
- to taste cherry jam

## Directions:

1. Leave the butter at room temperature for about 30 minutes to soften it. When ready, mix it with sugar in a large bowl. Add the egg and the vanilla extract and keep mixing with a whisk until frothy.

2. Add the flour, the salt, the sachet of baking powder and mix the ingredients. Continue to mix with the help of a spatula and finally knead all the ingredients by hand, just long enough to form a smooth, compact and homogeneous dough.

3. Wrap the dough with plastic wrap and let it rest in the fridge for at least an hour. Take the dough out of the fridge and roll it flat with a rolling pin. Use some flour to avoid sticking.

4. Coat the base of a baking tray with the pastry and put circles of pastry next to each other on the edges.

5. With the leftover pastry, form four cords and place them on the base of the tart, creating four sections that will house the jam. Put a piece of square pastry in the middle with Harry's initial letters (HP).

6. Pour the jams that we have chosen to use into the tart sections, creating a combination of colors you like.

7. To create the Harry Potter emblem we model all the elements and then we put them on top of the tart following the original model. Bake the tart in a pre-heated oven at 180° for 40 to 45 minutes.

# Recipe 18 - Harry Potter Pumpkin Howler

Another snack to try for the table. These are simple egg roll wrappers filled with creamy mascarpone filling but shaped in a nice Harry inspiring howler with icing eyes and lips drawn on the outside. Serve fresh and enjoy your favorite smoothies or drink in the evening.

**Serving Size:** 12

**Prep Time:** 10 minutes

**Total Prep Time:** 10 minutes

## Ingredients:

### Filling:

- ¼ tsp. cinnamon
- 1 Tbsp. brown sugar
- 2 Tbsp. pumpkin puree
- 8 oz. mascarpone cheese
- Pinch of salt
- Dash of nutmeg

### Howlers Wrap

- 3 egg roll wrappers, sliced in quarter pieces
- Red icing
- Black icing
- Oil for frying
- 1 beaten egg with 1 tsp. water (egg wash)
- 12 eggroll wrappers

## Directions:

1. Mix pumpkin with mascarpone cheese, cinnamon, salt, nutmeg, and brown sugar.

2. Spread the egg roll wrappers with their pointed side upward.

3. Add a Tbsp. of cheese is filling at the center of each.

4. Wet the edges with egg wash and wrap to form small envelopes.

5. Heat oil in a deep pan on medium heat.

6. Cook them in hot oil until golden brown.

7. Make eyes using black icing on each envelope and make lip using red icing.

8. Serve.

# Recipe 19 - Chocolate Spell Book

## Ingredients:

- 3 eggs
- 150 g sugar
- 250 ml Fresh liquid cream
- 250 g Flour
- 1 sachet Baking powder
- vanilla aroma

**Filling:**

- 250 ml Fresh liquid cream
- 200 ml condensed milk
- Raspberries
- Dark chocolate
- white nougat flakes
- 200 ml vegetable cream
- 200 g Dark chocolate
- 1 knob of butter
- sugar paste and powdered dyes

**Directions:**

1. Let's start with a rather simple base suitable for this type of recipe: it is soft and compact and lends itself to be stuffed.

2. Whip the eggs with sugar using whisks or a planetary mixer. Add the vanilla.

3. Sift flour and yeast and, when the mixture is clear and frothy, add them by spoonfuls a little at a time, until completely absorbed.

4. Whip the cream and incorporate it, with a spatula to the rest of the dough, with gentle movements from top to bottom so as not to disassemble the mass.

5. For this type of cake I used a 30 × 25 rectangular mold. Bake in a preheated oven at 180 ° for 30 minutes or more. To check if it's ready, do the

toothpick test before removing it: stick a toothpick in the middle of the cake and check if it is wet. If it's dry, the cake is ready. Let it cool.

6. Prepare the syrup by melting the sugar with water and maraschino in a saucepan over medium heat. This too will be have to be cooled when ready.

7. Whip the cream, prepare raspberries and dark chocolate flakes and when the cake is cold cut it horizontally into two layers.

8. Place it on the serving base and wet the first layer. Sprinkle with the filling, distributing the raspberries and chocolate. Overlap the other layer and bathe.

9. Fill with vegetable cream and put in the fridge for a couple of hours.

10. Now we can proceed with the decoration: here the choice is yours, if you have some manual skills you can easily try your hand at sugar paste, otherwise use the themed waffles and the pastry bag. The cake should be kept in the fridge until ready to serve it.

# Recipe 20 -   Molly's Pancakes

## Ingredients:

- Butter 25 g
- 00 flour 125 g
- Medium eggs 2
- Fresh whole milk 200 g

- Baking powder for cakes 6 g
- Sugar 15 g

For the syrup

- 1/4 cup butter
- 1/3 cup buttermilk
- 1/2 cup sugar
- 1/2 tsp. baking soda
- 1 tsp. butter extract (use vanilla if you can't find butter)

For the whipped cream

- 1 cup heavy cream
- 1/4 cup powdered sugar
- 2 tbsp butterscotch instant pudding mix (dry)

**Directions:**

1. We begin the preparation of the pancakes by melting the butter over very low heat and then letting it cool down. Meanwhile, divide the egg whites from the yolks. Pour the egg yolks into a bowl and beat them with a hand whisk, then add the melted butter at room temperature and the milk, while continuing to mix with the whisk. Whip the mixture until it is clear.

2. Add the yeast to the flour and sift everything in the bowl with the egg mixture. Stir well using the whisk to mix.

Now whip the egg whites you have kept aside, pouring the sugar little by little and when they are white and frothy, gently add them to the egg mixture, with movements from top to bottom, to incorporate as much air as possible. Heat a non-stick pan(don't use high heat, otherwise you will not give the dough time to rise well during cooking and the pancakes will become too dark) and, if necessary, grease it with a little butter. Pour a ladle of preparation into the center of the saucepan, there will be no need to spread it.

3. When bubbles begin to appear on the surface of the mixture and the base will have become golden brown, turn the pancake on the other side using a spatula, as if it were an omelette. When the other side will also have turned brown, the pancake will be ready. Continue cooking the remaining pancakes and gradually arrange them on a serving plate, stacking them on top of eachother.

Syrup:

4. While pancakes are cooking, add butter, buttermilk, and sugar to a medium sized saucepan. Stir the ingredients together on medium heat until all the sugar has dissolved and  the butter has completely melted. Boil the mixture for one minute and remove from heat.

5. Stir in the baking soda and butter extract. The syrup will now have a bubbly foam on the top: don't

worry, as this is completely normal. Let the syrup rest for a few minutes and it'll be ready to serve.

Whipped Cream:

6. Carefully whip all ingredients in a medium bowl until light and fluffy.

# Recipe 21 - Treacle Toffee Recipe

Make these black molasses toffees to serve on the table. These are made out of simple sugar mixture which mixed and cooled. Toffees can be stored in bite-size pieces in a sealed jar for days. Preserve in the refrigerator and serve whenever needed.

**Serving Size:** 6

**Prep Time:** 10 minutes

**Total Prep Time:** 10 minutes

**Ingredients:**

- 1lb dark brown sugar
- ¼ pint water

- ¼ tsp. cream of tartar
- ½ cup black molasses
- ½ cup corn syrup

## Directions:

1. Grease 30x10 cm pan with butter.

2. Mix sugar in water in a cooking pot over low heat.

3. Stir in all the remaining ingredients and bring it to a boil.

4. Pour this mixture into the greased pan.

5. Allow it to cool until firm.

6. Break the toffee into bite-size pieces.

7. Serve.

# Recipe 22 - Gillyweed Stalks

Health is always the first priority we all share as a parent. And there is no better delicious way to add zucchini to the home cuisine. Here the zucchini slices are seasoned and then grilled which gives it a strong aroma and earthly taste. Try these with your favorite dip or sauce.

**Serving Size:** 2

**Prep Time:** 10 minutes

**Total Prep Time:** 20 minutes

**Ingredients:**

- 2 zucchinis, sliced longitudinally
- 2 Tbsp. olive oil
- Garlic salt, to taste.

**Directions:**

1. Season the zucchini slices with garlic salt and 2 Tbsp. olive oil.

2. Refrigerate for 2 hrs. for marination.

3. Meanwhile, preheat a grill on medium heat.

4. Grill the zucchini slices for 2 minutes per side.

5. Serve.

# Recipe 23 - Golden Snitch Cake Pops

The golden snitch ball is what everyone is running after, at least in all the Harry Potter series. Today every Harry one is as much crazy about the snitch. These snitch cake pops are for all such lovers. These are made of simple cake recipes and then later coated with layers of pops, frosting, and customized lightning bolts.

**Serving Size:** 6

**Prep Time:** 10 minutes

**Total Prep Time:** 20 minutes

**Ingredients:**

- 1 tub store-bought frosting
- 1 box cake mix (+ required eggs and oil)
- Lollipop sticks
- Yellow candy melts
- White fondant
- Gold sprinkles (we bought this at Williams & Sonoma)

## Directions:

1. Make cake pops as per the given instructions on the box.

2. Roll the cake pops in the yellow candy melts. Allow it cool.

3. Coat the balls with gold sprinkles.

4. Using a sharp knife cut the wings out of white fondant.

5. Fix the wings in the cake pops and serve.

# Recipe 24 -  Hogsmeade Chicken Spindles

## Ingredients:

- 8 chicken spindles
- 50 g of butter
- 70 g of breadcrumbs
- 1 tablespoon of honey
- 1 tablespoon of soy sauce
- Salt

## Directions:

Place the chicken spindles in a bowl, pour the soy sauce and honey, then mix and leave to marinate for at least 2 hours. Drain the chicken drumsticks from the marinade and add salt. Melt the butter and brush the spindles well. Pass the buttered chicken drumsticks in the grated breadcrumbs. Line a baking tray with parchment paper, place the spindles on top and cook them at 200 ° C for 30-40 minutes. Serve the spindles hot.

# Recipe 25 - Bertie Bott's Every Flavour Beans

## Ingredients:

- 900 gr sugar
- 10 tablespoons lemon juice
- 10 tablespoons oranges juice
- 10 tablespoons blueberries juice
- 24 gr jelly sheets

## Directions:

Put the jelly sheets to soften in a bowl with cold water, leave it to soak for about ten minutes. Meanwhile, put 200 grams of sugar in a medium-sized saucepan, pour 10 tablespoons of lemon juice into it. Over medium heat, stirring, melt the sugar and bring to boil. When the first bubbles on the edges begin to form, turn the heat off. Squeeze the jelly sheets well and add them to the juice. Stir, it will melt in a few moments. Pour the juice into a dispenser with a spout, place your mold on a baking tray, fill each space completely. Gently put it in the refrigerator for about one and a half hours. Gently extract the jellies and roll them in the sugar. Repeat in the exact same way for the other two flavors.

# Recipe 26 - Quidditch Pudding

## Ingredients:

- Whole milk 200 g
- 00 flour 200 g
- Seed oil 140 g
- Eggs (about 4) 240 g
- Salt to taste
- Black pepper to taste

## Directions:

1. To prepare the yorkshire pudding, take a non-stick muffin pan and pour some seed oil inside, distributing it equally between the compartments. Insert the pan in the static oven preheated to 200 ° and heat the oil for about 15 minutes. In the meantime, add the eggs and milk in a bowl, add salt and pepper and mix with a hand whisk. When the eggs and milk are mixed, add the flour and mix again until a smooth and homogeneous batter is obtained.

2. After 15 minutes, remove the pan from the oven, being very careful not to burn yourself with the boiling oil and pour the batter into the compartments up to half their height.

3. Immediately put the pan back in the oven and continue cooking for about 30 minutes, without ever opening the oven. Once cooked, the patties will be beautifully swollen and then they will tend to deflate up to assume their characteristic irregular shape: let them cool slightly before turning out and serving your yorkshire pudding!

# Recipe 27 - Butterbeer Fudge Blondies

This is the perfect dish to make if you love the taste of butterbeer. Make these delicious blondies to satisfy your strongest sweet tooth.

**Serving Sizes:** 8 servings

**Cooking Time:** 40 minutes

**Ingredients for the blondies:**

- 1 pack of vanilla cake mix

- 2 eggs

- ½ cup of vegetable oil

- 11-ounce pack of butterscotch

**Ingredients for the fudge:**

- 11-ounce pack of butterscotch

- 1 can of buttercream frosting

- Powdered sugar, for dusting

**Directions:**

1. Prepare the blondies. In a bowl, add in the vanilla cake mix, eggs and vegetable oil. Stir well to mix. Add in the butterscotch and fold gently to incorporate.

2. Pour into a baking dish lined with a sheet of parchment paper.

3. Place into the oven to bake for 15 to 20 minutes at 350 degrees or until baked through. Remove and set aside to cool.

4. Prepare the fudge. In a bowl, add in the butterscotch. Melt in the microwave for 1 to 2 minutes or until smooth. Add in the buttercream frosting and stir well until evenly mixed.

5. Spread the fudge over the blondies.

6. Sprinkle powdered sugar over the top.

7. Slice into squares and serve.

# Recipe 28 - Monster Book Snacks

There are never-ending ways to make your cuisine look like Harry inspired and these monster book cookies are another way to nicely add an important part of the series to the table. These cookies are rich in chocolate, marshmallows, icings and graham crackers. Serve them with warm milk and the kids will love it.

**Serving Size:** 12

**Prep Time:** 10 minutes

**Total Prep Time:** 20 minutes

**Ingredients:**

- 24 graham cracker cookies

- 1 cup mini Marshmallow
- 1 cup melted chocolate
- ½ cup chocolate shreds
- ¼ cup M&Ms

## Directions:

1. Dip graham cracker in melted chocolate. Allow them to cool.

2. Spread icing on one side of the graham cracker.

3. Place marshmallows on the icing side of half of the graham cracker to make the teeth.

4. Place the remaining half of the graham crackers over the marshmallows with their icing side down.

5. Top the crackers with chocolate shreds.

6. Make book eyes with M&Ms and serve.

# Recipe 29 -  Beauxbatons Secret Recipe

## Ingredients:

- 1 carrot
- 1 onion
- 2 celery stalks
- lamb (ground) 500 g
- flour 2 tbsp
- meat broth 500 ml
- laurel 1 leaf
- tomato paste 1 tbsp

- potatoes 800 g
- butter 80 g
- milk 125 ml
- salt to taste

## Directions:

1. Wash the potatoes and place them in a large pot. Add plenty of salted water and cook for 15 - 20 minutes or until they are soft.

2. Peel the carrot and onion and cut them into cubes. Remove the filaments from the celery and chop it. In a large saucepan, add the oil and vegetables and cook on a low heat for 5 minutes. Add the lamb, cook until lightly brown and then add the flour and mix until the mixture is homogeneous. Continue cooking for 5 minutes.

3. Add the bay leaf, tomato paste and meat broth. Bring to a boil and continue cooking for 30 minutes, stirring occasionally. Season with salt.

4. Preheat the oven to 200 ° c. Peel the potatoes, mash them with a potato masher, add 50 g of butter, milk and mix. Season with salt.

5. In a large baking dish, arrange the meat and level the surface. Add the mashed potatoes and brush them with the remaining softened butter. Put in the oven and cook for 20 minutes. Serve hot.

# Recipe 30 - Polyjuice Potion Jelly Shots

Jelly shots are a fun way to incorporate Harry inspired recipe into your menu. These are colorful giggly delights which are made out of the delicious combinations of the ginger ale, pineapple juice, and lemon. They are great to serve as party snacks or a side dish on the dinner table.

**Serving Size:** 12

**Prep Time:** 10 minutes

**Total Prep Time:** 15 minutes

**Ingredients:**

- Ginger Ale mixture
- ½ cup ginger ale
- 1 envelope plain gelatin
- ½ cup ginger vodka
- Pineapple mixture
- ½ cup canned pineapple juice
- 1 envelope plain gelatin
- ½ cup pineapple vodka
- Lime mixture
- ½ cup water
- 1 envelope plain gelatin
- ½ cup lime sherbet, melted

## Directions:

1. Soak gelatin in ginger ale in a saucepan for 2 minutes.

2. Stir cook for 5 minutes on low heat then turns off the heat.

3. Add vodka and mix well.

4. Soak gelatin in pineapple juice in a saucepan for 2 minutes.

5. Stir cook for 5 minutes on low heat then turn off the heat.

6. Add vodka and mix well.

7. Soak gelatin in water in a saucepan for 2 minutes.

8. Stir cook for 5 minutes on low heat then turn off the heat.

9. Add melted sherbet and mix well.

10. Divide the three mixtures into silicone molds.

11. Allow them to cool and serve.

# Recipe 31 -   Chocolate Frogs

## Ingredients:

- 3 egg yolks
- 60 g of butter
- 300 g dark chocolate
- 100 g of sugar
- 7 tablespoons of bitter cocoa powder
- 80 g cocoa biscuits

## Directions:

1. First, whip the egg yolks with the sugar until a frothy mixture is obtained.

2. Afterwards, melt the chopped chocolate in a double boiler. Add the butter to the chocolate and then add the obtained chocolate cream to the yolk and sugar mixture.

3. Crumble the biscuits with the help of a rolling pin (or a food processor) and add them to the mixture. Now mix everything with a spoon and leave to rest in the refrigerator for at least an hour. At this point, unless you have a magic wand, you need to arm yourself with patience and stencils to give a shape to your chocolate. Leave in the refrigerator for a few hours, so that your chocolate can solidify. Be careful that Draco Malfoy's friends aren't around: they could make them disappear in seconds (and not with a wand).

# Recipe 32 - Hagrid's Rock Cakes

## Ingredients:

- 150 g sugar
- 130 g flour
- 2 eggs
- 180 g vegetable margarine (or butter)
- 130 g potato starch
- 1 sachet of baking powder (16 grams)
- 250g corn flakes
- 1 pinch of salt

## Directions:

1. Pour the margarine (at room temperature), the sugar and a pinch of salt in a large bowl. Stir the ingredients with the low speed electric whisk until a frothy mixture is obtained.

2. Add the eggs one at a time, while continuing to mix well with the whisk until the mixture becomes clearer and more homogeneous.

3. At this point add the flour, baking powder and potato starch, always mixing with the electric whisk. When the dough has taken on a beautiful smooth and compact appearance, put it to rest in the fridge for about 30 minutes.

4. After lining the dripping pan with parchment paper, pour the corn flakes into a large container. With a spoon, take a fair amount of dough and, after making a rough ball, roll it into the corn flakes, making sure that they adhere well to the surface, and flatten a little with your hands. Keep the shape a bit rough.

5. Arrange dough balls on the dripping pan, spacing them properly, and bake in a preheated oven at 180 ° for about 15 minutes (the surface must be golden brown in color).

6. Leave to cool and enjoy in good company!

# Recipe 33 - Pomphrey's Pumpkin Juice Smoothie

Who doesn't like a fresh dose of smoothie on a beautiful evening? This pumpkin juice is extra special due to its richness, color, and flavor. It has the added nutrients of apples, carrot, and orange alongside the pumpkin. It is simply great for the kids, and they would enjoy it on their Harry Potter theme celebrations.

**Serving Size:** 4

**Prep Time:** 10 minutes

**Total Prep Time:** 20 minutes

**Ingredients:**

- 1 cup cooked pumpkin puree
- ½ tsp. cloves, ground
- 2 carrot, chopped
- 1 tsp. vanilla extract
- 2/3 cup coconut milk
- 2 apples, peeled and cored
- 2 cup water
- 2 orange, peeled and cut into sections
- 2 bananas, peeled
- 1 tsp. cider vinegar
- 2 tsp. cinnamon

## Directions:

1. Blend all the ingredients in a blender.

2. Refrigerate for 1 to 2 hours.

3. Serve.

# Recipe 34 - Butterbeer Fudge

**Prep: 45 minutes**

**Serves: 4 Servings**

**Ingredients:**

- 1 3/4 cups sugar
- 3/4 Cup Evaporated Milk
- 7 Ounces Marshmallow Creme
- 1/2 Stick Butter
- 1 Cup Butterscotch Chips
- 3/4 Cup Dark Chocolate Chips

- 3/4 Teaspoon Rum Extract
- 1/4 Teaspoon Vanilla Extract

## Directions:

1. Line an 8-inch square baking sheet with parchment paper. Spread out the paper over the edges of the sheet.

2. In a heavy saucepan, pour the milk, sugar, marshmallow crème, and butter and cook over medium heat. When the mixture comes to a boil, reduce the heat and simmer for 3-5 minutes.

3. Remove the mixture from heat. Slowly add dark chocolate and butterscotch chips, about one-fourth cup at a time. Whisk until the chocolate and chips completely melted. Mix in the rum extract and vanilla.

4. Add the mixture to the pan and refrigerate until set.

5. Once the fudge has cooled and firmed, transfer to a cutting board and cut into squares. Store in an airtight container.

# Recipe 35 - Flaming Dragon's Blood cocktail

Hagrid's beloved dragon Norbert is the inspiration for this amazing cocktail. I like to garnish this drink with a spear of raspberries or slice of pineapple.

**Preparation Time**-5 minutes

**Servings** – 1

**Ingredient:**

- Blood Syrup
- 12 ounces frozen raspberries
- 3 sprigs of thyme
- 4 ounces white sugar
- 4 ounces of water

- Brown food coloring
- Cocktail
- 2 fluid ounces Bacardi Superior
- 1½ ounces blood syrup
- ¾ ounce lemon juice
- 2 ice cubes
- ⅛ teaspoon of Wilton Red Luster Dust
- 1/3 ounce rum

**Directions:**

**Blood Syrup**

1. Heat raspberries, thyme, white sugar and water in a saucepan on medium high heat.

2. Bring mixture to a boil, stirring constantly until sugar dissolves and raspberries are soft.

3. Remove from the heat and cool to the room temperature. Run syrup through a fine mesh sieve and pour syrup into a sealable container. Place in refrigerator.

**Cocktail**

1. Combine Bacardi, blood syrup, lemon juice, ice cubes, red luster dust and rum in a cocktail shaker. Shake vigorously for about 5 seconds and strain into a cocktail glass.

2. Place spoon on the surface of glass and layer blood syrup on the surface.

# Recipe 36 - Witches blood brew

The dry ice in this drink creates an amazing spooky atmosphere when activated by the liquid. Be extra cautious when handling dry ice as it can cause burns.

**Preparation Time**-5 minutes

**Ingredients:**

- 8 medium blackberries
- 2 ounces 100% agave silver tequila
- 1 ounce freshly squeezed lemon juice
- 1 teaspoon maple syrup
- 5 fresh sage leaves
- 1 dash orange bitters
- Blackberries
- Dry Ice

**Directions:**

1. Mix berries and sage in a shaker and muddle until fragrant and crumbled down.

2. Pour silver tequila, lemon juice, orange bitters and maple syrup in a cocktail shaker. Mix vigorously and pour over dry ice in a glass.

# Recipe 37 - Dark Lord cocktail

This drink might sound strong and foreboding, but it was designed by Voldemort after all. Serve this with some blackberries on a cocktail spear.

**Preparation Time-5 minutes**

**Servings – 1**

**Ingredients:**

- 1 ounce blackberry schnapps
- 1 ounce vodka
- 1/2 ounce cranberry juice

**Directions:**

Combine schnapps, vodka and cranberry juice in a drink shaker and shake vigorously. Strain mixture into a chilled glass.

# Recipe 38 - Pureblood Cocktail

The Weasleys were of pureblood as both of their parents contained mystical powers. I dedicate this cocktail to Ron Weasley and his family who always made Harry feel welcome.

**Preparation Time**-5 minutes

**Ingredients:**

- 6 ounces licorice liqueur
- 4 ½ ounces blackcurrant cordial
- 12 ounces water
- black food coloring
- 8 ounces sugar

**Directions:**

1. Pour water into a pitcher filled with water and add food coloring until desired colour is reached. Stir vigorously after every drop of food coloring.

2. Fill ice cube tray with black water and freeze until solid.

3. Combine 8 ounces of white sugar and ¼ teaspoon of food coloring in a large bowl and mix until completely incorporated.

4. Coat the rims of the glasses with black sugar. Fill each glass with a couple of ice cubes.

5. Mix liqueur, blackcurrant cordial and water in a large pitcher and pour into the glasses.

# Recipe 39 - Potter Pumpkin Cocktail

Pumpkins play an important role in the Harry Potter series. Whether being used as decorations, an excellent hiding place or an ingredient for pasties and juice, pumpkins make a delicious cocktail.

**Preparation Time**-5 minutes

**Ingredients:**

**Punch**

- 25 ¾ ounce spiced rum
- 8 ounces orange juice
- 8 ounces lemon juice
- 8 ounces spiced syrup
- 4 ounces pumpkin puree
- 20 ounces sparkling water
- cinnamon sticks

**Spiced syrup**

- 4 ounces demerara sugar
- 4 ounces water
- 6 whole cloves
- 6 allspice berries
- 1 cinnamon stick, broken into small pieces
- 1 star anise pod
- 6 white peppercorns
- 1/2 cracked nutmeg

- dry ice
- Hollowed out pumpkin

## Directions:

### Spiced syrup

1. Place cloves, allspice, cinnamon, star anise, peppercorns and nutmeg in a small pan and shake back and forth over medium heat to prevent them from burning.

2. Add water and sugar to the mixture as soon as the spices in the pan become fragrant and toasted. Keep stirring until the sugar dissolves completely.

3. Bring mixture to a simmer and reduce heat to low. Cook for 10 minutes more and remove from heat.

4. Strain syrup through a strainer and cool completely

### Punch

1. Combine spiced syrup, rum, orange juice, lemon juice, pumpkin puree and cinnamon sticks in a punch bowl safe for dry-ice.

2. Place a larger metal bowl in the hollowed out pumpkin and add dry ice to the bottom.

3. Pour punch through a strainer again and place in a bowl smaller than the bowl with dry ice

4. Place the punch bowl in the metal bowl. Stir punch and pour into small bowl.

5. Add sparkling water to the punch and stir.

6. Pour hot water into the metal bowl with the dry ice to activate it.

# Recipe 40 - Happy Elf cocktail

Noblepig.com

House elves are industrious characters in the Harry Potter series. Dobby, the house elf, is the inspiration for this cocktail when he became a free elf.

**Preparation Time**-5 minutes

**Servings** – 1

**Ingredients:**

- 2 ounces Absolut Citron vodka
- 1 ounce Midori liqueur

- 1 ounce white cranberry juice
- Maraschino cherries

**Directions:**

Place the ice in a cocktail shaker and then add all of the **Ingredients**. Shake very well until combined. Strain the cocktail in to a glass and top with a maraschino

# Recipe 41 -   Blood-sucking bat cocktail

This cocktail commemorates the bats released during the Final Quidditch Cup. The syringe injected with syrup creates an amazing image of blood.

**Preparation Time**-5 minutes

**Servings** – 4

**Ingredients:**

- 16 ounces frozen raspberries
- 2 ounces amaretto
- 2 ounces white sugar
- 4 ounces vodka

- 6 ounces club soda
- 2 ounces orange juice
- 4 plastic syringes

## Directions:

1. Place raspberries in a blender and process until pureed.

2. Place puree into a fine mesh sieve and press down to separate the seeds from the pulp. Discard seeds.

3. Mix raspberry puree with white sugar in a small pan on medium high heat.

4. Stir mixture often while it cooks until it is dark and thick. This should take about 10 minutes.

5. Place mixture in the refrigerator until chilled.

6. Combine amaretto, vodka and ice in a cocktail shaker and shake vigorously for 30 seconds. Add orange juice and club soda and stir. Pour into chilled glasses.

7. Fill a syringe with raspberry syrup mixture from the pan and inject into the cocktail before serving.

# Recipe 42 - Hair of Cerberus

I like to start with 3 ounces of gin and ¼ ounce of lemon juice when I want a drink that is lighter on the alcohol. Be very careful with the peppers, don't touch your eyes or lips after handling them unless you wash them thoroughly.

**Preparation Time**-5 minutes

**Servings** – 1

**Ingredients:**

- 1/2 ounce fresh lemon juice

- 3 dashes Tabasco

- 6 ounces Bulldog Gin

- 1 slice of chili pepper

**Directions:**

1. Combine gin and Tabasco in a cocktail shaker with ice and shake vigorously

2. Strain the mixture in to a cocktail glass and then top with chili pepper.

# Recipe 43 - Mudblood cocktail

Popular belief was that Purebloods were the most powerful of witches and wizards. This theory was disproven by Hermione, who was a mudblood and possessed superior qualities.

**Preparation Time**-5 minutes

**Servings** – 1

**Ingredients:**

- 1 ½ ounces Vodka
- 1 ½ ounces Baileys Irish Cream
- 1 ½ ounces Coffee liqueur

**Directions:**

Mix all **Ingredients** in a martini shaker with ice and shake vigorously. Pour liquid into a martini glass and top with coffee beans.

# Recipe 44 -  Witches Brew Punch

Amee's Savory Dish

Serve this delicious punch at your next Potter Bash and create a magical atmosphere. The green color and smoky appearance gives this drink a mystical aura when served.

**Preparation Time**-5 minutes

**Servings** – 2

**Ingredients:**

- 67.62 ounces chilled ginger ale
- 32 ounces chilled pineapple juice
- 2 ½ ounces freshly squeezed lemon juice
- 128 ounces lime sherbet
- 90 ounce block dry ice
- punch bowl that fit inside cauldron
- Large cauldron

**Directions:**

1. Wearing gloves, carefully break dry ice into pieces with a mallet. Place some dry ice in the cauldron and store the rest safely in a cooler. Pour hot water over the dry ice in the cauldron so it starts to smoke.

2. Place a bowl that is safe to use with dry ice on top of the dry ice in the cauldron. Mix ginger ale, pineapple juice and lemon juice in the bowl and mix well.

3. Add sherbet to the punch and stir gently until it starts to melt. Serve and enjoy!

Made in the USA
Monee, IL
01 December 2020

50433514R00069